Library of Congress Cataloging-in-Publication Data

Bosquet, Oscarine.
 [Poems. Selections. English]
 Mum is Down / Oscarine Bosquet ; translated from the French by Simone Fattal & Cole Swensen.
   pages cm
 ISBN 978-0-942996-82-1
 I. Fattal, Simone, translator. II. Swensen, Cole, 1955- translator. III. Title.
 PQ2702.O76A2 2013
 841'.92--dc23
                        2013038116

Original French: Mum is Down @ Al Dante, Paris, France 2012

Copyright © The Post-Apollo Press, 2014

The Post-Apollo Press
35 Marie Street
Sausalito, California 94965
www.postapollopress.com

Cover drawing by Simone Fattal
Book Design by Simone Fattal
Typeset by Lindsey Boldt in Cochin with
Desdemona & Century Gothic display

Oscarine Bosquet

MUM IS DOWN

**Translated from the French
by Simone Fattal & Cole Swensen**

THE POST-APOLLO PRESS

Sausalito, California

By the Same Author in English :

Present Participle, La Presse 2013 translated by Sarah Riggs and Ellen Leblond-Schrader.

1

Where are we when you pass

head in the gas stove
leaning over the window rail
the dosage
of the accelerator

against the plane tree
in the bay
the oven
the courtyard

in the courtyard the outline
of your body
fallen

leap
flight
fall

mom
me

Leap into the night at noon
the mother leaps
sudden void
ground
she leaps
crushes the afternoon
empty in no evening
the mother scattered
noon at night.

And the ground remains ground remains ground
                                      hard closed.

How long does it take a body to hit the ground
when it falls from I have no idea what height?

what did she have time
to think about what
as she was faster and faster falling
did she think also faster and faster
toward flight not toward the fall?

In her bosom detached the ribs
the hip-shape of her last
articulated sound
pokes through the cutting edge

A sound of bones remains
drawn as a mouth
turned inside out
toward the bitten teeth.

I blow on your bones so you can rise
between your lips my voice
rise up
in the wind
I blow my bones into your mouth
the flesh of my tongue.

The memory of the fall
your fall which drags me along
this decisive movement
after which we watch
the remains
288 bones.

In French the bones beneath the eyes are called
                                            pommettes
they are the little *pommes* of the *squelette*.

But on the other side the film sweeps her off
toward less cacophony
more stability
on the other side toward ascension
her arms looking for the sky
from the ground I fly
together far from the outline
on the ground of the fall.

Dance hanging
from the word fall
in memory you
hang I dance
with you dead.

Mom is down
The mother is
Down below
Mom
Mommy
Mummy's down.

*

Written in English in the original

2

The mother made of earth and water was gifted
                              with a voice

were you of water and blood?

the mother breaks
down water and earth
is in the landscape.

the mother is in the flowers
perennials all around scenting
water and earth where

lavender sage rosemary
I eat the strawberries over her
and leave the artichokes to bloom.

Lavender sage rosemary
small tomatoes and basil
eat mommy
eat me.

I put a piece of you in a bucket of water
a piece of you in water
so earth will grow
from a cutting
from your roots
dead in the landscape.

To take once more a single swallow of your voice
who is the one who is unstinting the subsong
clinging to the inverted glass?

You float drowned.

I drink her floating yellow a bit
a little more drowned each time
more yellow more abstract
each time more floating frozen
slicing the words
from her throat in a single sight
an endless stream from the same body
in the glass casket.

How much longer will she float?

3

Today has no more form nor
tomorrow frozen
into yesterday.

Gone in a single stroke.

She left no word
nor list of things to do
nor armies nor provisions
nor hiding place nor shelter
no template for the day
in the morning no trace
nothing nor for the afternoon
only a fall from noon into night.

How to deal with today?

How to deal with a beautiful day?
the glassy afternoon that stretches out into an end?

How to deal with today the snow melting under rain

and if the rain carries the landscape down into the ravine
and the ravine runs the slope into the slope
and the mountain mud into the river?

How many flowers have to grow together
to hold the landscape back?

How many stones must we leave in the garden's ground
to keep the landscape from running away?

In the garden that doesn't exist.
nor the trees above the bones
only the engraved stones.

How to find
The anchor how to
hold without slipping
from the heels to the eyes up
without buckling
without breaking turning
on the loosened axis?

Exactly where in time
do we start counting
the steps?

How to not melt in the falling snow?

To sew the beginnings of sunlit afternoons
with grey mornings without
falling
into the fog
going up or going down is the same
in the frozen vertigo
nothing pierces
crossing the white night of noon
slipping two feet facing
the slope up to the rock
after the hollow

evening sun.

Throwing stones ahead stones
To jump across
the time one doesn't touch the ground
from one to
the other
constructing
a ford
counting
from one foot to the other the steps
to move forward
jumpily sto
stoston
stone.

To find a form for the day
solidify the days by page
cut out pieces of morning
morning morninging noon night
then daypaging the content of the moon's tale
mars mercury jupiter venus sabbath master
to put the hours in the right order
one after the other
not on top of each other nor
leaving any space between.

4

Mommy are you the crafty wolf?
or are you the stepmother?
When the mother no longer wants the child
the stepmother sends her into the forest
mirror, mirror tell me who
who is the fairest
when the hunter makes the queen eat the heart of
                                        the doe
the young girl will only live with seven dwarves
does she believe in the prince's kiss which untangles
her from her mother's words.

To dance with the prince, the siren relied on the witch
and the mother drew her two legs with the slash
                              of a sword
  slicing the tail the length
  against the voice
  to dance with her prince
  what are you saying
  mute

  your legs beating the ground dancing two
  legs each step
  you're dying of pain
  mute
  the siren wrenches
  each step from the sea
  each step is a word that can no longer be said.

The two legs you gave me
are dancing on your voice mommy
are beating the ground without counting
dance two
legs one
mute box.

You left me a voice in my feet
so that each of your words resounds
echoes
the rhythm of your tender debris
articulates my bones to the hips
your bones
offset my steps
I limp
without understanding
the words danced in your bones
where my voice drowns in yours.

Mommy, are you the crafty witch?

Translator's Note :

Mum is Down was translated by Simone Fattal & Cole Swensen on July 17th and 19th and December 19th, 2012 at the Café de la Mairie du 6eme in Paris.

About the Author & Translators :

Oscarine Bosquet was born in 1964 in Paris. She is the author of four volumes of poetry in French and has published extensively in magazines and anthologies. She teaches at the Ecole Supérior des Arts in Brest. Her book, *Present Participle*, also in English, was recently published by La Presse.

A native of the San Francisco Bay Area, **Cole Swensen** is a poet and translator of French poetry, prose, and art critcism. She co-edited the Norton anthology *American Hybrid* and is the founding editor of the small press La Presse. She divides her life between Providence, RI and Paris.

Simone Fattal is a painter, sculpter and translator. She is the founder and publisher of The Post-Apollo Press.